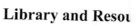

Warren Smith

London, New York, Munich, Melbourne, Delhi

Project Editor **Richard Gilbert**
Editors **Sophie Bevan, Kathy Fahey**
Project Art Editor **Mark Cavanagh**
DTP Designer **Vânia Cunha**
Production Controller **Elizabeth Warman**
Managing Editor **Stephanie Farrow**
Managing Art Editor **Lee Griffiths**

Photography **Melody Sky, Gerard Brown**

DVD produced for Dorling Kindersley by
Chrome Productions www.chromeproductions.com
Director **Robin Schmidt, Neil Gordon**
Camera **Neil Gordon, Gavin Rowe, Melody Sky**
Production Manager **Portia Mishcon**
Production Assistant **Gavin Rowe**
Voiceover Recording **Mark Maclaine**
Music **Chad Hobson**, produced by **FMPTV**

First published in Great Britain in 2006 by
Dorling Kindersley Limited
80 Strand
London WC2R 0RL

A Penguin Company

2 4 6 8 10 9 7 5 3 1

Copyright © 2006 Dorling Kindersley Limited

A CIP catalogue record for this book is available from
the British Library.

ISBN-13: 978-1-40531-617-0
ISBN-10: 1-4053-1617-9

Colour reproduction by Icon Reproduction, UK
Printed and bound in China by Hung Hing

Discover more at
www.dk.com

contents

10

how to use this book and DVD

This fully integrated book and accompanying DVD are designed to inspire you to get out onto the slopes. Watch all the essential techniques on the DVD in crystal-clear, real-time footage, with key elements broken down in state-of-the-art digital graphics, and then read all about them, and more, in the book.

Using the book

Venturing onto the piste for the first time can seem a daunting prospect, so this book explains everything you need to know to go skiing with safety and confidence. Cross-references to the DVD are included on pages that are backed up by footage.

Switch on the DVD

When you see this logo in the book, check out the action in the relevant chapter of the DVD.

Using the DVD

Supporting the book with movie sequences and computer graphics, the DVD is the perfect way to see key techniques demonstrated in precise detail. Navigate to each subject using the main menu, and view sequences as often as you like to see how it's done!

Flick to the book

When you see this logo on the DVD, flick to the relevant page of the book to read all about it.

why ski?

Skiing through fresh powder snow and making your way down mile upon mile of mountain terrain is probably one of the greatest ways that you can find to experience freedom. Skiing is a sport that rewards you for your perfections and punishes you for your mistakes, and it keeps you hooked because the surface you ski on is ever-changing, as is the mountain environment around you. From virgin powder snow off-piste to hard-packed groomed snow on-piste, skiing will give you many different challenges, constantly developing your physical and mental skills.

In this book, you'll learn about the basic principles of skiing. With technical procedures and exercises clearly explained and illustrated, you'll learn how to find your balance and steer from turn to turn in all types of snow and terrain with control and style. You'll also learn about the physical demands of skiing and find out how to strengthen the muscles that are most important to developing good skiing technique. Overall, you'll finish this book with a thorough understanding of one of the world's greatest sports.

Enjoy the learning experience and never tire of the quest for finding new and exciting descents!

coming up...

Clothing and kit: 18–33

Before hitting the slopes, you'll need to get the right ski clothing and equipment. The clothes you choose need to keep you warm, but must also be made from a breathable fabric that disperses excess body heat and moisture. Your choice of skis and boots will depend on your height and weight, skiing ability, and the terrain on which you'll ski.

Mountain safety: 34–37

The most important aspect of skiing is safety. Due to high altitudes, extreme temperatures, changing snow conditions, and the vastness of the mountain, it's important to do your safety homework before you start to ski. While on the mountain, always follow the rules of the piste and be aware of local information such as weather forecasts, piste maps, and avalanche warnings.

Pre-ski fitness: 38–43

Skiing is a sport that requires strength and endurance, especially when you're skiing at higher altitudes. Preparing the muscles used for skiing before you go will not only enhance your experience of the sport but also greatly reduce your risk of injury.

complete outfit

Having the right equipment and clothing is paramount to your safety and enjoyment on the slopes. To go skiing you'll need skis, boots, poles, bindings, technical outer layers of clothing, gloves, goggles, and a hat.

Getting kitted out correctly is something that you shouldn't compromise on when you go skiing. Perhaps the most essential items are the technical outer layers – your ski trousers and jacket. If you are not adequately dressed, you will suffer badly in extremely low temperatures. Ski boots being fitted correctly or not can make or break a ski holiday. Having the correct type and length of ski in relation to your ability and weight is also extremely important to your development and enjoyment of the sport.

Skis
Make sure your skis are suitable for your skiing ability, bodyweight, and height.

Bindings
Ski bindings can be adjusted for your bodyweight and ability. Get a professional to set them for you.

Trousers
Ski trousers should be roomy enough to let you flex and crouch down easily.

Poles
Your poles should be light and strong with a comfortable grip. They must have a wrist strap.

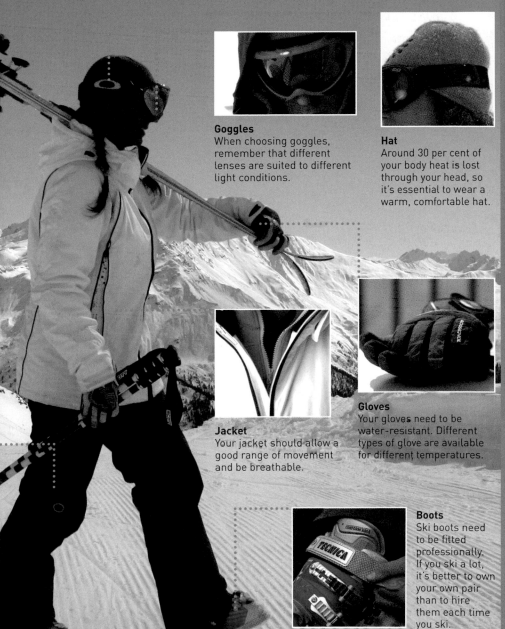

Goggles
When choosing goggles, remember that different lenses are suited to different light conditions.

Hat
Around 30 per cent of your body heat is lost through your head, so it's essential to wear a warm, comfortable hat.

Jacket
Your jacket should allow a good range of movement and be breathable.

Gloves
Your gloves need to be water-resistant. Different types of glove are available for different temperatures.

Boots
Ski boots need to be fitted professionally. If you ski a lot, it's better to own your own pair than to hire them each time you ski.

clothing

The cold temperatures of high-altitude mountain air and the warmth generated by the body during exercise mean that ski clothing has to provide both insulation and ventilation.

To keep warm on the slopes, you'll need a number of essential items: a ski jacket, ski pants or salopettes, a pair of padded gloves, a fleece or sweater, some thick ski-specific socks, and a hat. If it is particularly cold, you may want to invest in some thermal underwear.

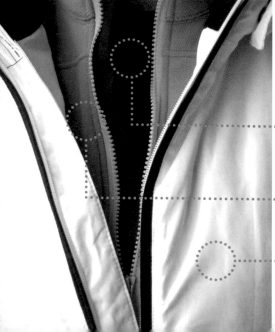

Layering basics

Skiers normally wear three or four layers of clothing to maintain the right temperature. It's better to wear a number of thin layers, rather than one or two thick layers.

Base layer

This is the most important layer and is often made of treated polyester. Look for a tight-fitting garment made from wicking materials that absorb and disperse sweat.

Mid layer

The mid layer should provide insulation. Often made of lightweight fleece, it must also be breathable to let moisture escape.

Outer layer

This layer is formed by the ski jacket and pants. As well as offering protection from wind and rain, it should also be breathable.

What to look for

There are a number of important features to look for when choosing ski clothing:

- Ski gloves need to be a snug fit to help maintain the right temperature. Ensure your gloves have a water-resistant membrane, and an elasticated band or strap near the wrist to prevent cold air or moisture getting in.

- Hats should be well-insulated.

- Ski socks are better than normal socks for skiing. The fabric is denser in the shin and sole to cushion shock, and thinner on the top to prevent bulkiness restricting movement.

- A snow skirt seals the bottom of your ski jacket, preventing snow from getting in.

- Heat-sealed zips and seams prevent water from seeping inside your outer clothing.

protective gear

When you ski, you need a certain level of protection from the elements. Even if you're skiing in great conditions on a day that is not particularly cold, you'll still need some protection. In low temperatures, in high or low light levels, when skiing at high speeds, or when skiing off piste, you'll need special protective gear. Wearing the correct gear when the conditions demand it can greatly reduce your risk of injury.

Essential protection

Ski goggles protect your eyes from sun, wind, and snow and are much safer than sunglasses, which can shatter if you fall at high speed. Gold reflective lenses are for sunny conditions, silver reflective lenses are for mixed light conditions, and orange lenses will help you to see in low light or cloudy conditions. A ski helmet protects the most vulnerable part of the body, your head, and greatly reduces the risk of serious injury if you fall.

Mixed light goggles   **Low light goggles**

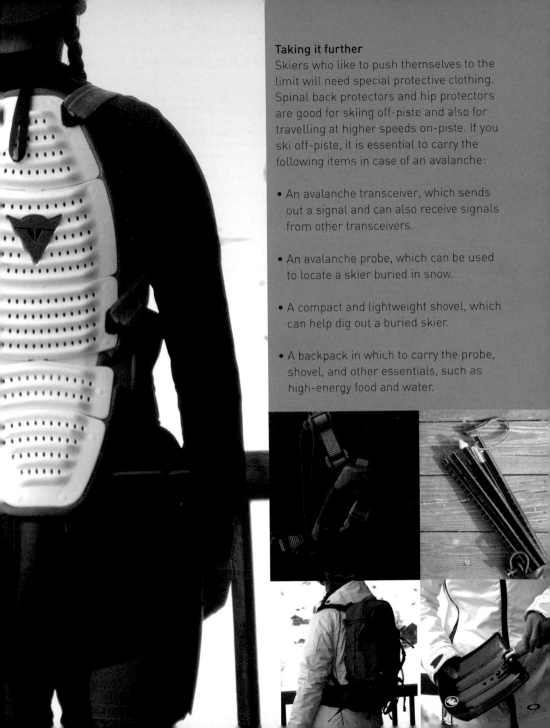

Taking it further

Skiers who like to push themselves to the limit will need special protective clothing. Spinal back protectors and hip protectors are good for skiing off-piste and also for travelling at higher speeds on-piste. If you ski off-piste, it is essential to carry the following items in case of an avalanche:

- An avalanche transceiver, which sends out a signal and can also receive signals from other transceivers.

- An avalanche probe, which can be used to locate a skier buried in snow.

- A compact and lightweight shovel, which can help dig out a buried skier.

- A backpack in which to carry the probe, shovel, and other essentials, such as high-energy food and water.

boots

Your ski boots are probably the most important items in your skiing wardrobe. They support your feet, and are the connection between your body and the skis.

It is essential that your boots are the correct size and shape for your feet. If they are too tight, they'll hurt while you're skiing, and if they are too loose, they won't give you enough leverage when you want to steer your skis.

Fitting boots

The best place to buy ski boots is a well-established ski shop, as they will have experienced staff and the correct equipment for fitting boots.

- Wearing your ski socks, stand up in the boot and do up the clips. If they need to be done up very tightly, the boot is probably too big.
- Your big toe should just touch the front of the boot.
- When flexing your ankle and pushing your shin against the tongue of the boot, your big toe should come away from the front of the boot.
- Your heel should be supported and should not lift up the boot as you flex your ankles forward.
- Ensure you can flex your ankle joint with a slow, progressive movement.

Boot construction
Ski boots are shaped to allow the skier to flex the boot comfortably. They usually come with a slight forward angle in the upper cuff.

Pressure strap
The pressure strap is used to help tighten the upper cuff of the boot, and give support to the calf.

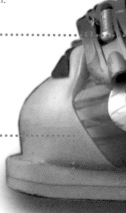

Outer shell
The outer shell is made of supportive materials that allow direct power transmission from the body to the ski.

Solid sole
The sole is made from a solid material and is designed to slot into the toe-piece of the ski binding.

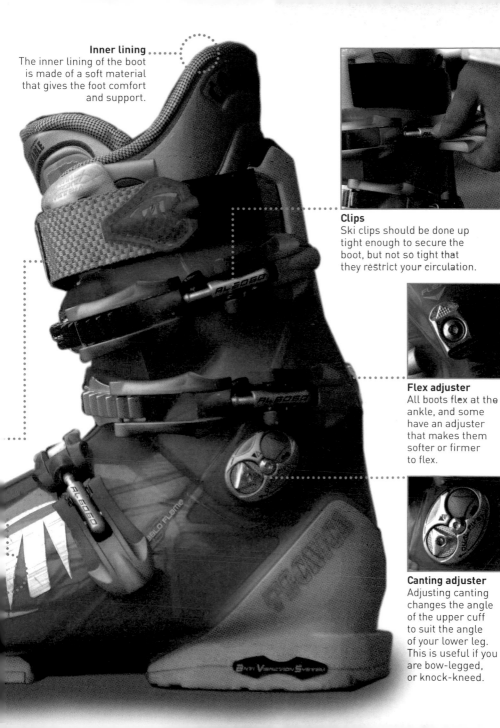

Inner lining
The inner lining of the boot is made of a soft material that gives the foot comfort and support.

Clips
Ski clips should be done up tight enough to secure the boot, but not so tight that they restrict your circulation.

Flex adjuster
All boots flex at the ankle, and some have an adjuster that makes them softer or firmer to flex.

Canting adjuster
Adjusting canting changes the angle of the upper cuff to suit the angle of your lower leg. This is useful if you are bow-legged, or knock-kneed.

how bindings work

Ski bindings attach your boots to the skis, and also convey the pressure you place on your boots to your skis, allowing you to steer them. Each binding comprises a toe-piece and a heel-piece, two brakes, and an anti-friction device. The bindings also incorporate springs that release your boots if the pressure on them becomes too great, so that the skis don't remain attached to your feet if you fall. This helps to reduce the risk of injury to your legs, especially your knees and ankles. Bindings must be adjusted correctly so that they release according to your personal criteria, such as height, weight, and skiing ability. This is best left to a qualified technician.

Toe-piece
Springs in the toe-piece release the ski if lateral pressure on it becomes too great.

Brake plate
Your boot presses down on the plate, lifting the brakes.

177 0610901

Anti-friction device
The smooth surface of the anti-friction device prevents the boot sticking to the binding if it releases.

Brake
The brake helps to prevent the ski sliding away if you fall over. It is spring-loaded, and will dig into the snow once your boot is released from the binding.

Boot in toe-piece
The toe of the boot slides into the toe-piece of the binding. The toe-piece and the front of the boot are made to fit neatly together.

Heel-piece
Springs in the heel-piece release the boot upwards if the skier falls forwards.

Catch
When you push your heel into the binding, the catch clicks upwards. Pressing down on the catch releases the boot.

Adjusting bindings
Ski bindings are set to release according to your height, weight, and skiing ability. They all use the DIN scale, which ensures consistency in settings. The settings can be adjusted with a screwdriver at the toe and heel. Always check your DIN settings with a qualified technician.

Boot in heel-piece
The heel-piece of the binding receives the heel of the boot and clicks down firmly to hold it in place on the ski.

ski technology

Far from being mere "planks of wood", skis are specially designed for optimum performance on the mountain. Modern-day skis are constructed using a combination of wood, metals such as titanium, and even carbon fibre. Also, many skis are now designed with an integrated binding system that improves the way they flex – all in pursuit of the best ride possible.

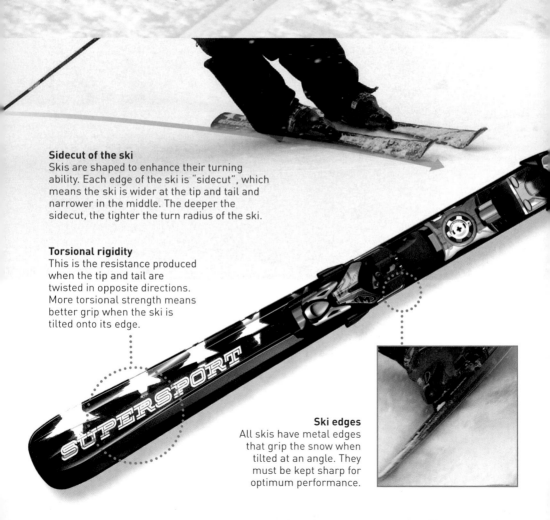

Sidecut of the ski
Skis are shaped to enhance their turning ability. Each edge of the ski is "sidecut", which means the ski is wider at the tip and tail and narrower in the middle. The deeper the sidecut, the tighter the turn radius of the ski.

Torsional rigidity
This is the resistance produced when the tip and tail are twisted in opposite directions. More torsional strength means better grip when the ski is tilted onto its edge.

Ski edges
All skis have metal edges that grip the snow when tilted at an angle. They must be kept sharp for optimum performance.

Base
The base of the ski is made with polyethylene. This allows it to glide on the snow with little resistance.

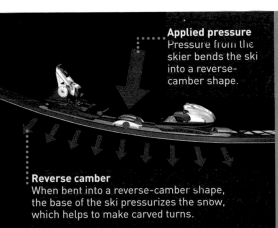

Applied pressure
Pressure from the skier bends the ski into a reverse-camber shape.

Reverse camber
When bent into a reverse-camber shape, the base of the ski pressurizes the snow, which helps to make carved turns.

Flex and camber
How a ski flexes varies depending on its type. Generally, skis for beginners are softer and easier to flex than those for advanced skiers. Skis are also designed with a camber, which means that the profile of the ski is curved up in the middle. When the skier applies pressure to the ski during a turn, the ski can be forced into a reverse-camber shape.

selecting skis and poles

An important decision you'll have to make when selecting equipment is choosing the correct skis. Factors to consider are flexibility – the more a ski can flex, the easier it is to manoeuvre; shape – the more exaggerated the ski's sidecut (see page 28), the more sharply it will turn; and length – the ski needs to suit your height, weight, and ability, and the terrain you plan to ski on.

Selecting ski poles

Ski poles consist of an adjustable, often aluminium, pole with a sharp tip and a basket on the base that stops the tip digging too far into the snow, and a grip and strap on the

top. You will find poles an invaluable aid to balance and timing as your skiing develops. To select the correct size, remember that you'll be taller when clipped into your skis, and the pole tips will be in the snow. For this reason, don't hold the pole by the handle – turn it upside down and hold it just below the basket. As you grip the pole, your forearm should be horizontal.

Types of ski

The type of skiing you enjoy will affect your choice of skis, since different designs are suited to different tasks. If you like carving at speed on piste, a stronger ski with a more defined hourglass shape will grip and steer more. If you want to ski deep powder, long, fat, big-mountain skis will help you ride through the snow.

Slalom ski .....
This short ski with a deep sidecut is ideal for shorter radius turns.

Giant slalom ski .....
Longer than a slalom ski and with less sidecut, this is best for larger radius, higher speed turns.

Twin-tip freestyle ski .....
This ski is easier to flex making it good for tricks and jumps. It can also be skied switch (backwards).

Big mountain/ .....
freeride ski
This is the longest ski with the least sidecut, so it's ideal for powder and variable terrain.

caring for and carrying your skis

Your skis will look better and last longer if you care for and carry them properly. There are several measures you can take to ensure that they stay in good condition.

The top sheet of your skis and their bases are vulnerable to damage, and can easily be scratched and dented. Be careful not to cross the tips or tails of your skis and avoid other skiers when side-stepping up a hill and manoeuvring.

The bases of your skis and their edges should be maintained by professionals in a ski shop, but you should dry them with a soft cloth after your day's skiing. If water dries on the skis time after time, the base will become less slippery and will slow you down. Wet metal edges can corrode, reducing their ability to grip the snow.

Using a Velcro strap to hold your skis together when carrying them also helps keep the edges sharp. Carrying skis and poles correctly reduces wear on them, and also reduces the risk of hitting other people with them.

1 Carrying skis
Before picking up your skis, turn them on their sides and push the bases securely together. Then, ensuring that you are gripping both sides of the skis, pick them up using both hands.

Other ways to carry skis

Skis can also be carried under your arm or over your shoulder. To do the latter, rest the skis on your shoulder with the front of the binding just behind your shoulder. Raise the tails of the skis high so they don't obstruct other people.

2 Once you have them upright, push the ski that is slightly higher downwards so that the brakes lock together. This holds the skis together.

3 Lift the skis by holding them underneath the toe-piece of the lower ski and pulling upwards and inwards to your chest. Keep the skis pressed against the body.

4 Take your poles in your free hand. As you begin walking, try not to rush. Remember that ski boots are quite slippery.

rules of the piste

When you ski, you should always observe the rules and signs on the mountain to help keep yourself and others safe. If you take the time to look, you'll notice that ski resorts are full of signs that give directions, show you the level of difficulty of pistes, and warn you of hazards. You should also observe the ten rules shown opposite.

Every established resort produces a map that shows you a scaled-down version of the mountain you'll be skiing, with all the pistes marked according to their location and difficulty (green, blue, red, and black – see page 155), as well as the locations and types of the lifts you'll be using. This is called a piste map and you must always take one with you when you ski. You can pick one up when you buy your lift pass. The piste map will also have a detailed explanation of the resort's signs and what they mean.

Safety rules

The International Ski Federation (FIS) has ten safety rules:

1. Skiers must not endanger others.

2. Speed must be adapted to personal ability and conditions.

3. Skiers in front have right of way.

4. Overtaking is allowed, provided that there is enough space.

5. When entering a marked run, skiers must check uphill first.

6. Skiers must not stop in narrow places or if visibility is restricted.

7 Skiers on foot must keep to the side.

8. Skiers must respect all signs and markings.

9. Skiers are duty bound to assist at accidents.

10. In an accident, skiers must exchange names and addresses.

staying safe on the mountain

Skiing is a sport that is all about fun, action, and enjoying the mountain environment. However, like many action sports, it does carry with it an element of risk. To stay safe while skiing you need to be aware of the snow conditions, the weather, and perhaps above all, your own ability.

Altitude and conditions

Skiing is usually done at high altitude. This can cause temperatures to be lower, winds to be higher, and sunlight to be stronger. You should prepare for these factors by making sure that you wear the correct clothing, the appropriate ski goggles, and a high-factor sun cream and lip balm. High altitude can also put more strain on your body and may make you feel faint, lose your appetite, feel sick, or have a headache. Make sure that you drink plenty of plain water throughout the day and bring a few energy bars in your ski jacket pockets to help you avoid fatigue.

During a week's skiing, you could encounter several types of snow. Depending on temperature, weather, time of year, altitude, the direction the slope faces, and time of day, you could be skiing in powder, ice, slush, or crusty snow. Take advice from an instructor or the ski patrol so that you ski on snow that is safe for your ability, and not likely to avalanche. A blue run can become as difficult as a black run (see page 155) if the conditions change from groomed piste into slush that's freezing into ice.

Watching the weather

It's important to be aware of weather conditions as you ski. At high altitude, the weather can change very quickly from one extreme to the other. If the weather is deteriorating rapidly, finish your run and stop skiing. Always take avalanche warnings seriously.

What to do in an accident

- Protect the casualty from being hit by other skiers and ensure they are secure, then use your skis to make a cross in the snow as a warning to other skiers.
- Check for life-threatening injuries such as unconsciousness, bleeding, or lack of breathing or pulse.
- If you don't have a first-aid certification, ask if someone at the scene does before

trying to help the casualty yourself.
- Don't attempt to move the casualty in case of back or neck injuries.
- Keep the casualty warm and comfortable.
- Alert the ski patrol. Get their number when buying your lift pass, but if you can't telephone, send someone to the nearest ski lift, where staff will be able to radio for help.

why get fit for skiing?

Although skiing is a recreational sport that's usually done on holiday, it's important to recognise the physical demands it puts on your body. To perform the movements necessary for skiing, your muscles need to be in good shape. You should also be aware of the stress that might be placed on your joints.

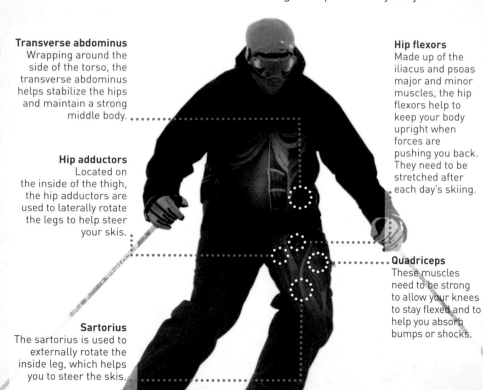

Transverse abdominus
Wrapping around the side of the torso, the transverse abdominus helps stabilize the hips and maintain a strong middle body.

Hip adductors
Located on the inside of the thigh, the hip adductors are used to laterally rotate the legs to help steer your skis.

Sartorius
The sartorius is used to externally rotate the inside leg, which helps you to steer the skis.

Hip flexors
Made up of the iliacus and psoas major and minor muscles, the hip flexors help to keep your body upright when forces are pushing you back. They need to be stretched after each day's skiing.

Quadriceps
These muscles need to be strong to allow your knees to stay flexed and to help you absorb bumps or shocks.

Muscles used for skiing

While skiing you'll notice certain muscle groups and areas of your skeleton working harder than others. These areas (highlighted below) need to be trained and exercised. The lower back, core, and leg muscles all need to be in good condition. Use the exercises on pages 40–43 to prepare your muscles for skiing, maximize your performance, and reduce your risk of injury.

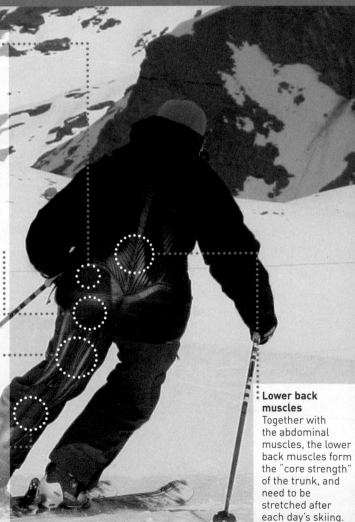

Gluteus medius
Found beneath the gluteus maximus, this muscle helps to rotate the skis and extend the legs while steering.

Gluteus maximus
The biggest muscle in the buttock, the gluteus maximus is the most important hip extensor muscle, and works with the hip flexors to help you keep a solid posture.

Hamstrings
Your hamstrings are used to aid knee flexion and shock absorption.

Gastrocnemius and soleus
These muscles are important for boot flexing. Stretch them after skiing to maintain full flex.

Lower back muscles
Together with the abdominal muscles, the lower back muscles form the "core strength" of the trunk, and need to be stretched after each day's skiing.

pre-ski exercises

Getting fit for skiing before you set off on your skiing trip is essential, so make sure you add these exercises for your calves, hips, and legs to your fitness routine. Begin two months before your trip and aim to do them every other day if you can.

Exercising your calves
Tight calves can make it hard to flex your ski boots. Place one foot in front, keeping the rear heel on the ground, and slowly lunge forwards. Hold for 20 seconds. Repeat three times on each leg.

1 Exercising leg-steering muscles
Many skiers lack the strength to steer with their legs. Lift one leg and move your knee across your body, without twisting your hips.

2 Steer your thigh all the way across your body, until you have reached the full range that is possible for you without your hips twisting.

1 **Exercising hip joints**
This exercise helps your thighs to rotate. Place your hands on the top of your hips to help stabilize them.

2 Move your feet to the left until you reach the limit of movement, keeping the hips facing forwards. Use your hands to oppose rotation of your hips.

3 Move your feet in the opposite direction, thinking about rotating your thighs. Repeat the exercise 20 times.

3 Then extend the thigh outwards, keeping the foot of this leg next to the knee of the supporting leg as you do so. You can feel your leg-steering muscles working.

4 Reach your maximum outwards range, then allow the foot to drop. Do 25 rotations. Repeat the exercise three times with each leg.

warming up and warming down

It's essential that you perform a good warm-up routine and equally important to warm down afterwards by stretching. Skiing for prolonged periods may cause muscles to tighten, which can put stress on your lower back and make it difficult to flex your ankles. To warm up your muscles, ski gently for 15 minutes, then do each of the three warm-ups twice. At the end of your day's skiing, make sure your last run is a gentle one, then do each of the four stretches twice, ideally within 20 minutes of stopping skiing. Don't over-exert yourself – the duration and repetitions of exercises can vary according to your fitness.

a Warming up quads and hamstrings
Slowly lift your leg forwards and backwards 20 times, using your poles to balance. Don't swing the leg at all – use your muscles to lift it. Keep your upper body still, ensuring your hips don't swing.

b Warming up your thighs
Balance on your poles and lift your knee in the air, placing your boot on the opposite knee. Move your leg across your body so it's under the opposite shoulder, then move it back. Repeat 25 times on each leg.

c Warming up your core muscles
Lie on your back with your knees bent. Pull your core muscles in and push your lower back into the ground. Straighten one leg, then raise and lower it slowly. Repeat ten times, then switch to your other leg.

d Stretching your hamstrings
Slowly lower your body onto your rear knee, extending your front leg. Feel the stretch along the back of your front leg, and hold it for 20 seconds. Then switch to your other leg.

e Stretching your glutes
Lie on your back and raise your knees. Place one foot on top of the opposite knee, and slowly pull that foot towards your chest. Hold it for 20 seconds, then switch to your other leg.

f Stretching your lower back
Lie on your back and pull one leg across the other, bending at the knee, while stretching your upper body in the opposite direction. Hold for 20 seconds, then switch to your other leg.

g Stretching your hip flexors
Kneel down with one leg bent forwards and slowly bend the front knee, allowing the hips to move forward. Feel the stretch at the top of your rear leg. Hold it for 20 seconds, then switch to your other leg.

WATCH IT
see DVD chapter 1

go learn the basics

coming up...

Finding your feet: 48–63

In your early days of skiing you'll need to get yourself booked into a ski school, so that you learn the basics correctly and safely. Ski-school tuition will help you get comfortable with standing on skis and using ski equipment, as well as helping you develop posture, balance, and the basic skills you'll need to move about on the beginner's slope.

Snowploughing: 64–71

One of the big achievements in your first days of skiing will be learning to control your speed. The snowplough wedge not only allows you to control your speed but also forms the basis for making your first turns. It's a technique that you will find useful far beyond your first weeks of skiing.

Moving around the mountain: 72–75

Once you've mastered the snowplough and feel confident making snowplough turns, you can start to access more of the mountain's vast terrain. You'll start moving higher up the mountain and will use the ski resort's system of lifts. This is when the real fun begins!

finding a ski school

Ski coaching is essential for your first few weeks of skiing. You cannot and should not attempt to get started without it, so when you're planning your skiing holiday, it's important to arrange tuition at a ski school in the resort you'll visit. Being part of a group in your first week or two of skiing is also a great experience that you will remember for years.

Many skiers stop ski-school tuition once they have the ability to make basic parallel turns. This often leaves them stuck at one level of ability. To really open the door to carved turns, steep terrain, moguls, and freeskiing, you need to continue with ski coaching. It makes skiing more fun and also reduces the risk of injury.

Points to consider
- If you are learning from a foreign-language instructor, ensure they speak your language well and have a good understanding of skiing terminology.

- In ski-school classes, try to make sure your group size does not exceed ten people.

- Try to book your skiing lessons before you arrive at the resort to guarantee your tuition and take the stress out of your stay.

- If you don't understand a technical explanation, ask your instructor to explain in more detail.

- If your instructor has gone out of his or her way to help you, it's customary to offer a tip.

- Remember that you always have the right to complain if you are not satisfied.

Children

Skiing lessons for children are run in a slightly different manner from skiing lessons for adults. Children's groups usually wear brightly coloured bibs so they can be easily identified on the mountain, and the classes focus on learning through games and friendly competitions, such as races. Many resorts also have specific children's ski playgrounds, with fun features that help to keep the children entertained.

getting into your bindings

1 Putting on your skis
Clean any snow off the base of your boot by rubbing the bottom of the boot against the toe-piece of the binding. Use your poles to support yourself while doing this.

2 Push the toe of your ski boot into the toe-piece, making sure the sole of the front of the boot fits under the wings of the binding cover and is straight along the ski.

1 Taking off your skis
To take off a ski, look at the heel-piece and aim the tip of your ski pole into the hollow groove in the top.

2 Put your weight onto the ski pole to push down on the heel-piece and lift the heel of your ski boot as the binding releases.

Putting on and taking off skis may seem daunting the first time you do it, but there are a few easy techniques you can learn that will help. Your ski boots slot into bindings, which are screwed to the skis. The bindings have tension springs inside that hold the boot in place but that release if you fall, allowing your foot to come free of the ski, which reduces the risk of injury.

3 Look at the back of your boot and line up the heel in the cup of the heel-piece, It's important that your foot is straight on the ski.

4 Once you're sure both toe and heel are straight on the ski, push your weight down into your heel until it clips solidly into the binding.

Practising sliding

To get a feeling for sliding on snow, try moving around with just one ski on and the other foot free. This will help you develop your balance and will also prepare you for going downhill. Choose a flat area or very gradual slope to practise. Use your poles to support yourself and put your weight onto the leg with the ski on. Lift up your other leg and get a sense of how it feels to balance like this as you move on one ski. Walk and slide along like this for a minute or two until it feels comfortable, then take this ski off, put it on the other foot, and do the same thing with your other leg.

adopting a dynamic stance

A dynamic stance is extremely important in skiing because it's a sport where the terrain is constantly changing. The slope you ski down will not be perfectly smooth but will have contours, and you will need to adapt to them.

The body in the dynamic stance

While skiing in the dynamic stance, each part of your body has an important part to play:

- **Head** – the more level your head is, the better your balance will be.
- **Shoulders** – your shoulders should usually be rounded, but they can be lowered for high-speed carved turns on-piste, and raised higher for moguls and off-piste terrain.
- **Lower back** – a rounded lower back absorbs shocks and helps to maintain correct hip position.
- **Hands** – your hands can make constant slight adjustments to help you maintain balance.
- **Hips** – the area around your hips is the centre of your mass, so it carries a lot of weight when you're skiing.
- **Knees** – the knee joints flex to maintain balance, but overflexing them can cause you to lose balance.
- **Ankles** – flexing your ankles allows your knees to flex naturally.

Head
Hold your head up and level, and look forwards.

Hands
Keep your hands in front and slightly out to each side, but still in your field of vision.

Dynamic stance in action

As the skier descends, the position of his body and flexibility of his joints ensure that he stays in constant balance. His dynamic stance also enables his legs to have the strength to steer even when countering the pressures generated by his speed. Without a dynamic stance, he would soon fall.

Lower back
Round your lower back as if slightly crouching.

Shoulders
Keep your shoulders rounded and not hunched.

Knees
Flex your knees to help maintain your balance.

Hips
Activate your core muscles to keep your hips over the balls of your feet.

Ankles
Flex your ankles, which will also help your knees to flex correctly.

WATCH IT
see DVD chapter 1

using the ankle flex test

Being able to flex your ankles when skiing is essential. All the flexing joints in the legs (the ankles, knees, and hips) need to flex equally to keep the hips hovering over the balls of the feet. This puts the legs in a position where they have the leverage necessary to steer.

1 Testing for ankle flex
Once you are clipped into your binding, make sure your ski boots are clipped securely and comfortably around your foot. Extend your ankles until you are standing as straight as you can comfortably be.

2
Slowly flex the ankles and feel your shins press down against the tongue of your boots. As you're flexing down make sure that the movement is progressive.

Quite often when people learn to ski, they lack the ability to flex their ankles adequately. Beginning skiers may also bend their knees too much. If your ankles are not flexed enough and your knees are bent too much, you will ski out of balance. In this position, it is much harder to steer the skis correctly using the legs.

3 Make sure that you keep your hips over the balls of your feet as you flex. Your knees should move over the toe-pieces of your bindings and your boots should continue flexing to their limit.

WATCH IT
see DVD chapter 1

How not to do it
If you can't flex your ankles sufficiently, you will end up bending your knees too much, which forces you to sit back over the skis. This makes it difficult to steer.

skating

A great way to get a feel for the edges on your skis and how they can support you is to skate with them on the flat. It's also a good way to warm up before you start skiing downhill and is a useful technique for moving across flat areas of snow with a minimum of effort. Skating on the flat is similar to skating on ice or inline skates, so if you have done either of these before, you may find it easier.

1
Skating on the flat
Start with your skis pointing in the direction you want to travel. Grip your poles firmly, plant them in the snow in front of you and give yourself a strong push off.

2
Using your right ski as a firm base, push out and back with your left ski, propelling yourself forwards.

1 **Gripping your poles**
To grip your poles correctly, slide your hand through the pole strap so it rests loosely around your wrist.

2 Then bring the grip of the pole towards the palm of your hand. Make sure that it's facing in the right direction so that you don't grip it backwards.

3 Grip the pole using all four fingers. You can rest your thumb over your forefinger. This position makes it harder to lose a pole if you fall.

3 You will now be sliding forwards on your right ski. Bring your left ski back into parallel alongside the right.

4 Repeat the process, this time pushing out with your right ski. Keep planting your poles for support and propulsion.

WATCH IT
see DVD chapter 1 ▶

making your first descent

Your first actual downhill run on skis will involve three techniques – side-stepping, pivoting around your poles, and straight-running. This method of ascent and descent is the safest way of getting started and will instil the most confidence. Choose a gentle nursery slope with a long, flat run-off that will bring you naturally to a halt. Ascend the slope by side-stepping, then pivot your skis safely until you're facing downhill, before enjoying your first descent.

1 Side-stepping
Face your skis across the slope (perpendicular to the fall line – the path a ball would take if rolled down the slope).

2 Move your uphill leg up the slope, approximately half a metre (1½ ft) above you. Keep using your downhill leg for support and grip.

3 Keeping the uphill ski on its uphill edge, lift the downhill ski up the slope to join it. Repeat this process until you have ascended.

1
Your first descent
Once you have side-stepped up the slope, you must turn your skis to face down the fall line. Plant your ski poles just downhill of your position.

2
Transfer your weight onto the poles, using your palm to press down. Then step your skis around in a wedge shape, which will support you and help stop you sliding on your skis.

3
Once you are pointing downhill, step the skis into parallel to get in position for your first straight run. Remember to check that your path is clear before setting off.

4
Release your weight from your poles and allow your skis to slide. Maintain a dynamic stance and raise your head to look in the direction of travel.

Place your hands in front of you to help stay balanced.

Bend slightly at the knees.

Flex your ankles in your ski boots.

WATCH IT
see DVD chapter 1

getting up

One thing that is sure to happen sooner or later during your skiing career is falling over. If not done correctly, getting back on your feet can take a lot of unnecessary energy and put undue pressure on your joints. Like most things, however, getting up is easier with experience. To take the strain out of getting up, follow these easy steps to ensure success without too much effort.

1 Standing up
Remain lying on your side and pull your feet up towards your hips. This brings your centre of mass closer to your feet so that it's easier to get up. Once you've got into this position, bring your shoulders up and use your stomach muscles to sit up slightly.

2 Check your position on the hill. To get up successfully, your skis need to be pointing across the hill, not down it. Adjust their position if you need to. Then bring your poles up beside you and get a good grip on the handles, digging your pole tips into the snow.

3 Push yourself up using your poles. As you're doing this, keep trying to lean your shoulders and head forwards. As your hips come up off the snow, keep using the poles until you get fully upright.

drills for balance and movement

As you're learning to slide on your skis, you'll benefit from practising drills that develop your feeling for balance while moving. The sooner you learn to flex and extend your legs, rather than keeping them in one position, the better. Working on your balance when you learn to ski will give you a sound basis for developing your technique later on. To help you get started, try the following drills.

a Boot flexing
As you begin your straight-running descent, slowly flex your ankles by pressing your shins down on the tongues of your boots. Repeat this from the start to the finish of your run. Keep your hips over the balls of your feet.

b Lifting feet alternately
When you learn to turn, you will feel different pressures building against each foot. A good way to prepare for this feeling is to lift your feet up and down alternately while sliding along the snow.

Touching boots

It's a good idea to get used to moving around on the skis by standing up and crouching. As you slide along, crouch down and touch your boots, then stand up as tall as you can. Repeat for the duration of the run.

Jumping

You can test your balance further by jumping. Flex down onto your boots and then extend upwards rapidly until your skis leave the ground. When landing, flex through all the joints in the leg, especially the ankles.

c

d

WATCH IT
see DVD chapter 1

creating a snowplough

A snowplough is a wedge shape that helps you control your speed, and is also used when you begin learning to turn. When you push your heels outwards to form the wedge shape, the skis are automatically tilted onto their inside edges. It's the edges as well as the ski shape that help to control your speed.

Try the snowplough position first on the flat. Jumping, brushing, and stepping your skis into the wedge shape can all be used to get your muscles working, and will familiarize you with making the snowplough.

a Brushing into a snowplough

The best way for the beginner to move into the snowplough shape is to brush the tails of the skis outwards. Stand with your skis parallel and plant your poles. Push your heels away from you, trying not to brush too far at first, and form the wedge shape with your skis.

b Jumping into a snowplough

Once you're familiar with the snowplough wedge, adopt the shape by actively working your legs. Grip the poles to support yourself and jump your legs outwards. Try to move your ski tips inwards and your heels outwards as you do this.

Anatomy of the snowplough

Symmetry is essential in the snowplough. If your body is shifted to one side, it will affect your direction of travel. Check that your eyeline is level, your shoulders are level, and that your hands are at an equal height. Try to keep the angles of both skis matched.

Head
Keep your head up and look forwards in the direction you're travelling.

Knees
Keep your knees flexed slightly, but not too much. Overdoing it will throw out your balance.

Edges
The skis should be on their inside edges.

Ankle flex
Your ankles should be flexed equally. This will help your other joints flex.

Ski tips
Your ski tips should be about 15 cm (6 in) apart.

WATCH IT
see DVD chapter 1

snowplough speed control

By changing the angle of your snowplough, you can increase or decrease the speed of your descent. A narrow snowplough shape will make you go faster, while a wider snowplough will make you go slower. The wider apart your skis are in the snowplough, the more your edges will be angled and the more resistance your skis will have against the snow. You can use this principle to stop while descending. Doing this will help to develop your control and will also build your confidence.

1 **Braking with a snowplough**
Adopt the dynamic stance and begin gliding in the snowplough position in a normal position, keeping your ski tips approximately 15 cm (6 in) apart.

2 Progressively brush your feet wider apart, but make sure that you maintain the same distance between the ski tips throughout.

Skis are flat

Skis are angled

WATCH IT
see DVD chapter 1

3 As you're brushing the skis wider, allow your hips to drop a little. This increases the skis' tilt on their edges, creating more resistance and stopping your descent.

Arms forward

Practising speed control

Try practising your snowplough to control the speed of your descent. Begin by straight-running on the beginner's slope, then brush your heels out into a wedge and feel your speed decrease. Before you come to a halt, allow your skis to come back into a parallel position and feel your speed increase again. Repeat this several times as you progress down the slope.

snowplough turning

Once you can brake in the snowplough and stay symmetrical on your skis, the next stage is snowplough turning. Stay on the same gradient of slope as you used for braking. This will be one of the first times that you will feel a difference in pressure on your left and right skis. As you turn your skis across the hill, the force of gravity will pull your body down the fall line. So, if you're turning left, you will feel an increase in pressure on your right (outside) ski.

Sweet spot
Check that your ankles are sufficiently flexed to bring your centre of balance over the balls of your feet, so that your skis will pivot around this point, or "sweet spot". It's important that your bodyweight is not over the back of your skis. If it is, the tails of the skis will dig into the snow and stop you from turning.

Ankle flex

Sweet spot

Ankle flex
The correct degree of ankle flex will help you keep your hips, and hence bodyweight, over the balls of your feet. This makes turning possible.

2 Begin your turn by steering your left ski to the right. Feel the ski pivot around the ball of your foot. Maintain the wedge.

1 Practising snowplough turns
Start with your body facing down the fall line. Check that your weight is equally distributed on both feet, your wedge is even, and the ski tips are about 15 cm (6 in) apart.

4 As you end your turn, your speed will decrease. Keep your wedge and use your braking technique if you don't come to a definite stop.

3 As you turn, pressure will build against the left (outside) ski. The pressure will reduce on the right (inside) ski.

WATCH IT
see DVD chapter 1

steering with the thigh

Before progressing too far with your snowplough turns, it's essential to learn to use the muscles in your legs to steer the skis. Thigh steering is by far the most effective and safe way of steering.

Most skiers begin by steering their skis using their feet, but this is a weaker method than thigh steering and puts stress on the knees. Steering from the thighs allows you to rotate the skis smoothly and reduces rotation of the upper body, which you must avoid to stay balanced.

Use your muscles
The muscles that are used to rotate your legs are the sartorius and piriformis for the inside leg, and the gluteus medius, gluteus minimus, and adductor muscles for the outside leg (see pages 38–39).

The hip adductors are used for steering the outside leg.

The leg muscles, such as the sartorius (on the inside leg), must be active in the turn, or the turn will be weak and place stress on the knees.

1 Exercising thigh-steering muscles

Support yourself by leaning on your ski poles. Then lift one of your legs and drive the knee across your hips until it's above your other knee.

2

Drive your knee back across your body and rotate it out to the side. As you do this, keep your foot close in under your knee until you have finished the rotation. Repeat 20 times on each leg.

Avoiding upper body rotation

Most people instinctively want to steer by rotating the upper body, especially the shoulders and head. If the upper body does rotate, it will increase your speed and cause you to lose balance when trying to steer through your turns. Be aware that thigh steering will help you avoid this happening. You can also try to think about keeping your hands, shoulders, and head level as you turn.

linking snowplough turns

When you're comfortable turning in both directions, try linking your snowplough turns together. To do this, use the same slope gradient as you did when practising single turns (see pages 68–69). Once you can link turns, you'll be reaching an exciting new stage in your skiing development. You can venture onto the green and blue runs of your chosen resort and really begin to explore.

Feeling a pedalling motion

As you begin to link your snowplough turns together, you will notice a pedalling motion in your legs. As in the action of pedalling a bike, when the outside leg of the turn extends, the inside leg flexes. At the start, allow an equal amount of pressure to return to your legs between turns, to re-centre in the fall line.

2 To begin the turn, add pressure on the right ski by extending your right leg, and reduce pressure on the left ski by flexing your left leg. Use your thighs to steer into your desired turn shape.

4 Repeat the pedalling action to increase pressure against the outside ski, and reduce it against the inside. Actively steer with your thighs to bring the ski around the turn.

1 Before initiating your first turn, feel equal pressure between the skis, with the tips 15 cm (6 in) apart. Your hips should be over the balls of your feet.

3 Before you start to turn back the other way, make sure you return to the centre. Then shift the pressure onto your left leg to initiate the new turn.

Different turn shapes

You can make your linked turns wider or narrower according to the gradient of the terrain, the snow conditions, or your personal preference. The wider the turn, the more exaggerated the pedalling and steering are, and the more you must steer with your thighs. Wide turns are slower than narrow turns.

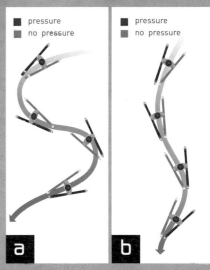

■ pressure
■ no pressure

■ pressure
■ no pressure

a

b

a **Wide turns**
The heavily steered turn shown above would be used on steeper gradients, or on faster snow conditions. It's also useful for skiers who need to build up their confidence.

b **Narrow turns**
This narrower turn is typically used on shallow gradients, or on heavy, slow snow. Skiers who enjoy travelling faster would use a narrower turn such as this.

drag and chair lifts

The main types of lift you will use are drag lifts (such as button lifts and t-bars) and chair lifts. Beginner areas usually have drag lifts, but as soon as you start going further up the mountain you'll need to use chair lifts as well.

There's nothing difficult about using lifts as long as you keep a few basic principles in mind. The most important thing to remember when using a drag lift is that you cannot sit down on it. You have to stand up, balance, and be dragged – it's a bit like skiing uphill. When getting on a chair lift, it's important that you look behind to see it coming. Once you're on, keep a firm grip on your poles.

Chair lifts

To get on a chair lift, turn and watch as it approaches and prepare to sit down. Once you're sitting, reach up and pull the safety bar down and place your skis on the ski rest below your feet. As you approach the top, take your skis off the rest and raise the safety bar. As your skis touch the snow, stand up and ski off immediately.

1 Using a drag lift
Hold both ski poles in one hand. When signalled to move forward, grab hold of the next pole and position it between your legs.

2
Shuffle your skis forward through the small barrier that activates the lift. As you wait for the lift to extend, ensure your skis are parallel and your joints are flexed, and prepare for a jolt as the pole extends.

3 As the pole extends and starts pulling you uphill, make sure you stand up. Keep looking ahead to ensure that your skis are parallel and stay in the tracks made by previous skiers.

4 As you approach the end of the lift and the ground flattens, pull the pole down between your legs and let it go. Move away from the lift as quickly as you can to avoid being hit by the next skier.

go ski parallel

coming up...

Preparing to ski parallel 80–91

To progress towards parallel skiing, you need to become confident and strong in your snowplough turns. Once you've achieved this, you can prepare for parallel skiing by getting a feeling for the edges on your skis using the traversing and side-slipping exercises. You also need to focus on the steering action in both legs to get your skis turning together.

Matching your skis: 92–95

As your skis move from the snowplough wedge shape to making turns in parallel, you will discover a smoothness and ease to your skiing. Parallel skiing requires you project (or move) your bodyweight at the beginning of a turn and to steer your legs progressively throughout the turn. At this stage in your skiing you need to be steering with your thighs and separating the upper and lower body.

Pole-planting: 96–99

To add further stability and confidence to your skiing, you'll need to use your poles. Pole-planting is the action that gives you up to four points of contact with the snow. It's especially important when you're making tighter turns, and gives greater rhythm and balance to your parallel skiing.

how and why to ski parallel

The next stage after linking your snowplough turns is to develop your technique into parallel turns. Parallel turns are more effective and more efficient than snowplough turns, because in a parallel turn your skis work together, rather than in opposition to each other.

This means that you have two ski edges gripping the snow for you rather than one. A snowplough wedge only allows one edge to grip the snow when you turn, making it a less effective means of turning on slippery terrain or in powder or heavy snow. In parallel, when you move on to skiing in powder or heavy, ungroomed snow, your skis will be able to cut through the snow simultaneously.

a Skiing in parallel
By making a parallel turn with your legs at the same angle, the skis can match and travel together, making them more effective for gripping, skidding, cutting through powder, and skiing steep terrain.

b Skiing in snowplough
When making a snowplough turn, your legs are asymmetrical and the ski edges are not matching. Only one edge is supporting you. If left to glide on their own, the skis would travel in different directions.

a

Legs aligned
The distance between the thighs, knees, and feet is equal.

b

Legs diverging
The distance between the thighs, knees, and feet is unequal.

Anatomy of parallel skiing

Notice the position of the skier's body in a typical parallel turn, with his hips level and weight balanced over the balls of his feet. Notice also how the skier's upper and lower body move independently of each other, with the legs leaning as the body remains vertical.

Upper body
The shoulders and hips are level and face down the fall line.

Thighs
The muscles in the thighs steer, with rotation in the ball-and-socket hip joint of the hips.

Ankle flex
The ankle joints are flexed, helping to maintain balance through the turn.

Parallel skis
The two skis travel together at the same angle.

traversing and side-slipping

Learning to traverse gives you a feel for how the skis' edges grip and support you on the hill. Side-slipping, one of the most important skills you can learn, will let you manoeuvre down steep slopes without excessive lateral movement or speed.

The aim of traversing is to gain distance across the hill without dropping or skidding sideways. As your technique progresses, the side-slipping technique can be used to help take the speed out of parallel or carved turns that may be accelerating too fast. It's also very useful for getting down narrow sections of terrain and negotiating moguls.

1 Traversing
To begin, set yourself up with your skis across the hill, in a position where they don't slide forwards. Lean into the hill to tilt the skis onto their edges.

2 Use your poles to help push you along, and start traversing across on your edges. Maintain your leg lean to keep the skis tilted on their edges.

3 Travel for a few metres first. As you become more skilful, travel for a longer distance. Always check above you for skiers on the piste.

How not to side-slip

Many skiers feel intimidated about bringing their hips over their feet to flatten the skis and release the edges. The feeling of slipping causes many skiers to lose confidence, so they tend to keep their upper body away from the downhill side of the slope. Doing this automatically puts skiers off-balance, and can sometimes cause their skis to slip backwards down the hill. To avoid this happening, follow steps 1-3 carefully, and make sure that your movements are as smooth and progressive as possible throughout the exercise.

1

How to side-slip
Begin by making sure your hips are slightly uphill, so that your skis are tilted securely onto their edges.

2

Then slowly move your hip down the hill so that it is more on top of your feet. Encourage your downhill ski to flatten. The ski edges should release and slip.

3

To stop the side-slip, simply revert to your starting position, moving your hips back up the hill.

Shoulders
Keep your shoulders parallel with the skis.

Eyes
Look down the hill, in the fall line.

WATCH IT
see DVD chapter 2

Downhill ski
The edge of this ski grips the snow.

working your inside leg

Your inside leg is always the one on the inside of the turn, and developing its steering action is one of the most important aspects of progressing your turn from snowplough to parallel. This leg is usually under-worked so you need to train it to help you through the turn – the drill below will make the steering action of your inside leg proactive, rather than just active, allowing the skis to become parallel earlier.

1 Thigh-steering drill
Leave your poles by the side of the piste and set off down the slope. Begin to make a snowplough turn and place your inside hand on the inner thigh of your inside leg.

2 Gradually pull and rotate the thigh outwards with your hand. This will help encourage your thigh to rotate at the hip joint, which encourages an early steering movement.

3 As your thigh rotates throughout the turn, your skis will draw parallel naturally. This should leave you in a symmetrical stance that allows your skis to cut through the snow.

WATCH IT
see DVD chapter 2

Inner-leg thigh steering

To progress your snowplough into parallel with strength and confidence, start to use your thighs to rotate the skis. The thighs contain some of the body's strongest muscles and are the key to powerful steering of your skis.

Rotate the thigh

The thigh begins rotating outwards when the downhill ski is supporting more of your bodyweight.

Steer the inside ski

The action of the thigh allows the ski to rotate and start the progression towards matching the skis into parallel.

Match both skis

The result of this thigh-steering is matching skis, and a symmetrical stance that uses two ski edges to support the turn.

J-turns

Making a J-shaped turn is a great way to get a feel for parallel skiing. As the name suggests, you set off down the hill and make a turn after gaining speed in the fall line. The turn is more complete than a simple snowplough turn and ends up with your skis actually pointing slightly uphill. The J-turn is an exercise that also enhances the position that your body should be in while parallel turning. This makes it a good way to experience the sensation of parallel turns before you actually start doing them.

Using J-turns to experience parallel skiing

As you pick up speed in the fall line, your body's momentum will become a stronger force. When you begin to turn your skis across the hill, this force will pull your bodyweight down the fall line. This causes the pressure to build up on the downhill ski and automatically makes the uphill ski lighter. As you continue steering across and back up the hill, the uphill ski will continue to feel lighter and lighter, so it can be moved easily into parallel.

J-turn tips

• As ever, balance is crucial. Stay in a relaxed position throughout, with your hips over the balls of the feet and your ankles flexed.

• Build up some momentum, but don't try to go fast at first. It's easier to keep control of the turn at lower speeds.

3 Keep steering the new downhill ski across the hill. Your uphill ski will want to rotate to match the downhill ski.

1 How to do J-turns
Turn your skis into the fall line and narrow the size of your wedge to increase speed slightly.

2 Steer your outside ski across the hill, feeling pressure build as it becomes the downhill ski.

4 As you steer across the hill, maintain the flex in your joints. Let your uphill ski be relaxed and light.

5 Rotate your uphill ski to match the downhill ski. Feel how the two skis skid together at the end.

WATCH IT
see DVD chapter 2

using rhythm to get parallel

By now, you have learned several techniques that allow you to control your skis. Adding rhythm to your turns is the next step towards parallel skiing. You can develop rhythm by aiming to make your turns within an imaginary corridor 3–4 m (10–13 ft) wide. Having to turn within this space will help you to move with a more progressive and rhythmical feeling.

Developing a pedalling action

By turning within a "corridor" of a constant width, your legs will instinctively begin to perform a pedalling motion as the pressure transfers from one ski to the other. As this feeling increases with the rhythm of the turns, you'll feel a greater confidence in applying more pressure to the downhill (outside) ski and reducing pressure off your uphill (inside) ski. The pedalling action that your legs perform is very similar to the way you would pedal a bicycle – the outside leg extends while the inside leg lifts. The earlier in the turn the pedalling action takes place, the earlier your inside ski will match the outside ski and become truly parallel.

5 Use the pedalling action to aid early pressure change, so your inside ski lightens and steers in the fall line.

1 Moving into parallel
Start off your series of turns in the snowplough position.

2 Towards the end of the first turn, feel your inside leg start to soften and steer.

3 With increased rhythm, you can encourage your inside leg to soften earlier, bringing the skis closer to parallel.

4 As one turn finishes, immediately start to prepare for the next. Avoid traversing the slope and losing your rhythm.

7 The skis are now matching parallel. With early pedalling it is possible for you to achieve parallel turns.

6 Good rhythm and pedalling will help to bring your skis parallel.

WATCH IT
see DVD chapter 2

steering from the legs

One of the most common mistakes that skiers make is to try to turn with no upper and lower body separation. This means that the skier turns the whole body in order to turn the skis, and it usually happens when the skier is out of balance and not skiing efficiently. The best way to turn your skis is to steer your legs independently of the hips and upper body. When you do this, the ball of the hip rotates inside its socket, allowing the legs to steer across the slope while the hips and upper body remain facing down it.

Pole window drill
Use your poles to create a "window" looking down the slope. Look at the "view" through the poles and ski down the slope, turning but keeping the view the same. This will encourage your legs to steer independently of your upper body.

Hands on hips drill
By placing your hands on your hip bones, you can feel whether your hips are rotating in the turn. Having the support of your hands can also help stabilize the hips and promote good leg-steering with correct rotation.

1

Parallel turns with leg steering
As you begin to turn, aim your upper body and hips at something in the fall line that's straight in front of you. This will help you keep your upper body facing downhill throughout the turn.

Rotation of the shoulder
The skier incorrectly rotates the shoulder to initiate the turn.

2

As the steering progresses, use the thigh muscles to steer the skis. The hip joints rotate to allow your upper body to remain facing downhill as your legs do the turning.

No separation
The skier rotates the whole body just to enable turning the skis.

3

As the rotation increases, steer with your leg muscles to finish the turn. Because the ball of the hip has rotated inside the socket, it will now want to return to its natural position. This will help you flow naturally into your next turn.

WATCH IT
see DVD chapter 2

Loss of balance
The skier's body position has thrown his hip out and flattened his skis, so they skid.

moving into parallel

Making your first parallel turns is a great feeling. Steering in both directions with the skis matching feels smoother, and when performed correctly, actually takes less energy than turns made using the snowplough wedge shape.

To achieve complete parallel turns, you need to add two extra elements to your skiing: mid-body projection and progressive steering. Mid-body projection means being able to move your hips forwards and across, to help both legs move and both skis tilt simultaneously. Progressive steering means being able to complete the turns smoothly and evenly, in a rhythmic pattern.

1 Turning in parallel
At the initiation of the turn your hips will be over the outside edge of the skis. The edges are still engaged from the previous turn.

2 As your hips project across and forwards, your weight shifts your skis simultaneously onto the new inside edges and they begin to turn.

How not to parallel turn
If you steer too suddenly, whipping your skis around instead of being progressive, your smooth S-shaped turns will become sharp Z-shaped turns. Too much pressure can build up on the skis' edges, forcing them to skid out of the arc of the turn. The outside ski may break into a wedge, causing you to lose the parallel ski position.

3 Continue to steer progressively through the turn, steering from the legs and not the upper body.

4 Your turn should progress smoothly through an arc shape. Both skis need to keep the same angle until you begin the next turn.

WATCH IT
see DVD chapter 2

ankle flex exercise

After learning to ski parallel, many skiers move on to more advanced techniques without making full use of their ankle joints. This can cause problems, because if you flex your knees and hips but not your ankles, your knees may overflex and cause you to "sit back" over your skis, throwing you off-balance.

1 **Flexing your ankle**
Plant your poles firmly in the snow to support you, and lift your downhill leg. Test the flex in your uphill ankle joint before your start.

2 With your poles still supporting you, start to flex and extend the uphill ankle so that it makes you hop. Keep the downhill leg raised.

3 Continue hopping on your uphill leg, turning in a half-circle, ensuring that the ankle joint flexes each time you land.

A lack of ankle flex also gives you less leverage for steering your skis. A flexed ankle makes the leg a much stronger steering lever, which gives you extra power, which in turn builds confidence. The ankle flex exercise is a great way to develop flexibility in your joints. It will also show whether your skis boots are flexible enough.

4 When you come to point down the fall line, be careful not to allow your weight to drop back over your skis.

5 Continue hopping and rotating on one ski, focusing on keeping your ankle flexed and using your thigh, not your foot, to do the turning.

6 When you finish, keep the leg in the air briefly before dropping it down. Repeat the exercise with the other leg.

pole-plant fundamentals

Once you've developed your skiing level beyond basic parallel turns, you'll soon discover the importance of the pole-plant – a stab into the snow with your ski poles at the beginning of a turn.

The pole-plant is an important aid to timing – keep your pole-plant rhythmic and your turns will be rhythmic too. The poles also provide extra points of contact with the snow, adding a level of balance and dynamism to your skiing, which you will find essential when it comes to steeps, moguls, and freeskiing.

O-frame arms

Maintaining an oval-shaped arm posture in the upper body gives you more power when the pole is planted. This reduces the risk of upper-body rotation, which can unbalance the skier, as the forearm is less likely to rotate outwards.

A-frame arms

Many skiers adopt this upper body posture. However, if you pole-plant in this position, your forearm will swing out further to the side. This makes the upper body rotate, which in turn rotates the hips and unbalances the skier.

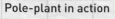

Pole-plant in action
The pole is being planted into the snow at the start of a turn. Both the poles are constantly moving – as soon as one is planted, the other moves forwards to prepare for the next turn. The pole acts as the third point of contact between the body and the snow.

Curved arm position
Maintaining an oval arm posture keeps the upper body strong and stable.

Centre of gravity
The pole-plant helps project the centre of gravity forwards and downhill in the turn.

Skis flat
As your hips cross over your feet, the skis move from right-hand edges to left-hand edges.

Pole forward of body
Position your pole diagonally in front and downhill of your new inside foot.

practising pole-planting

Pole-planting in the basic parallel turn is reasonably straightforward. It's when your skiing becomes more demanding – with steeps, moguls, freeskiing, and higher-tempo turns – that a stronger pole-plant becomes necessary. Skiers trying to increase their pole-plant strength often make the mistake of swinging their arms up and down in an attempt to increase the power of the plant. To develop the strength of your pole-plant correctly, work on the following techniques. They are designed to stabilize your arms and improve the power of your pole-plant.

1 Positive pole-planting
Before impact, use your left wrist to swing the pole diagonally forwards into an angled position.

2 Using the O-frame posture you've been practising, angle the pole for maximum strength on impact.

3 Begin moving your right wrist, ready for the next plant, and maintain your O-frame arm position.

Wrist movement

A strong pole-plant comes from a small flick of the wrist – the movement does not come from swinging the arms. Standing still, practise moving the pole backwards and forwards with the wrist only. When it feels right, try the exercise while skiing.

4 Try to angle the pole so that the basket is ahead of your hand. This will increase the power of impact.

5 On impact, keep driving the wrist forwards and downwards to help maintain the shape of the O-frame posture.

6 Work the left-hand wrist to manoeuvre the pole into the correct angle for the next plant.

go carving

coming up...

Discover carving: 104–107

Skiing down the mountain involves various forces. Gravity pulls you down the slope, while centrifugal force pulls you away from the direction in which you are turning. Carving is all about learning to manage the different forces you and your skis are under, and learning to use the shape of your skis to maximize your carved turns.

Carving skills: 108–111

Improving your carving technique involves learning to lean your legs further inside the turn and steering more progressively to develop the dynamics of your carved turns. Doing the exercises given on these pages will help you improve your carving technique.

Refining your technique: 112–115

When you are able to carve, you can begin travelling at higher speeds. However, when you travel at these speeds you will need to be more sensitive to the increasing pressure that will build up under the skis' edges. As your technique becomes more precise, any imperfection in your stance will become more noticeable. A strong, symmetrical stance is needed for clean carved turns.

the science of carving

A carved turn uses the shaped edge of the ski to cut a clean arc through the snow with a minimum of skidding. Being able to make carved parallel turns brings a new level of enjoyment to skiing, as you learn to use ski technology and the forces at work on your body to your advantage.

Carved turns can vary quite a lot depending on the shape (sidecut) of your skis. A deep sidecut will almost carve an arc shape for you. Less sidecut means that you have to do more of the work yourself to turn the skis.

The ease of carved turns
In new powder, the trail of this skier's carved turns can be seen very clearly. He is capitalizing on the physical forces present when skiing to make his turns, which means that he is able to ski with less effort and more enjoyment than if he were making basic parallel turns.

Tug of war
In a carved turn, you will feel pressure against your ski edges as the force of your weight builds up while travelling outwards in the turn. To control this force, you use your body to lean inside the turn. To get a feeling for this position, ask a friend to pull on your arm while stationary and counteract this simulated force by leaning your body over into the turn.

Forces in action

As the skier steers through a turn, he creates centripetal force by leaning inside the arc shape his skis are making. This prevents his body from being pulled outside the arc by the opposing centrifugal force. The force of gravity pulling the skier down the hill is opposed by the skier steering his skis across the hill and absorbing the build-up of pressure with his body.

Centrifugal force

This is the force that acts on your body by trying to throw you outwards when you're steering into a turn.

Centripetal force

This is the force your body applies when it leans inwards, putting the hips inside the arc of the turn, to counter centrifugal force.

Gravity

This is the force that pulls your body straight down the fall line and keeps you moving.

Pressure from snow

The pressure of snow against the skis must be carefully controlled by the skier, according to speed, terrain, and conditions.

WATCH IT
see DVD chapter 3

using the skis' sidecut

Skis with a deep sidecut (exaggerated hourglass shape) will make tighter turns than skis with less sidecut.

Slalom skis have far deeper sidecuts than freeride skis, so have a shorter turn radius. Simply standing on a ski increases the arc shape and lowers the turn radius, producing tighter turns. It's a good idea to get a feel for your skis' turning ability before taking on any carved turns. You can do this by practising the railing drill, outlined below.

Railing drill
To feel your skis' turning ability, choose an almost flat area of terrain. As you start sliding down the fall line, let your hips move laterally across the skis. Don't apply any leg-steering or pedalling action to the turn. Allowing the skis to glide on their edges will show you their turning ability.

Tilted skis ....
Tilt the skis onto their edges, so the skis are only turning with their sidecut. The skier here is not steering or pressuring the skis.

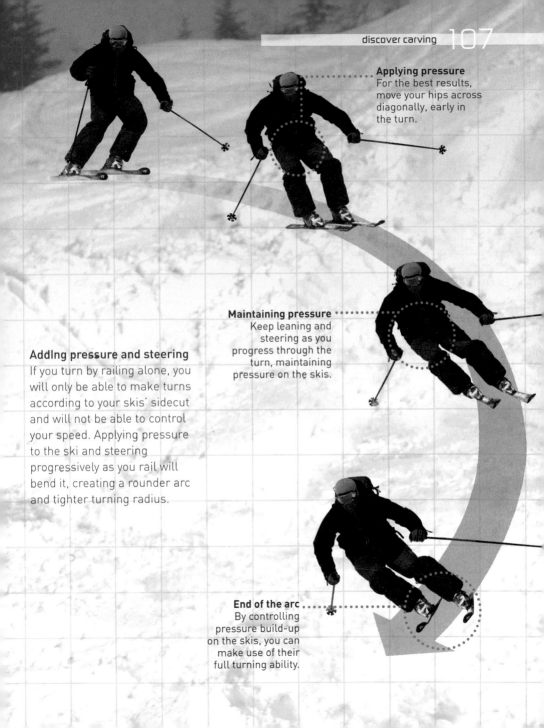

Applying pressure
For the best results, move your hips across diagonally, early in the turn.

Maintaining pressure
Keep leaning and steering as you progress through the turn, maintaining pressure on the skis.

Adding pressure and steering
If you turn by railing alone, you will only be able to make turns according to your skis' sidecut and will not be able to control your speed. Applying pressure to the ski and steering progressively as you rail will bend it, creating a rounder arc and tighter turning radius.

End of the arc
By controlling pressure build-up on the skis, you can make use of their full turning ability.

developing dynamic angles

If you want to travel faster and make more dynamic turns, you will have to resist greater centrifugal force. To do this, your hips need to be further inside the turn and your ski edges need to be more angled.

Many skiers never reach their full potential in carved turns due to an inabilty to lean far enough into the turn. This inability is often both physical and psychological. The area of the body that is often restricted is the hips. Doing the drills shown opposite can help you overcome this restriction, as well as any fear of falling that may be inhibiting you.

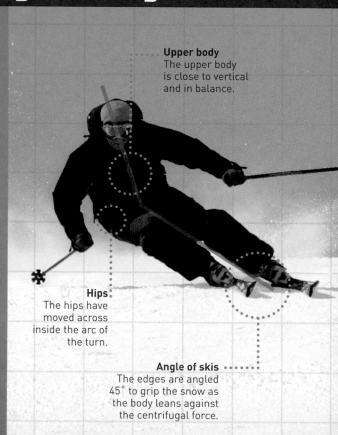

Upper body
The upper body is close to vertical and in balance.

Hips
The hips have moved across inside the arc of the turn.

Angle of skis
The edges are angled 45° to grip the snow as the body leans against the centrifugal force.

Hip-encouragement drill
To lean the legs, you need to move your hips laterally. As you turn, put your hand on your outside hip and push it into the turn. This will move the hip inside the turn and increase leg lean and edge angle. Then try to repeat the drill without using your hand.

Use your hand to push your hip inside the turn.

a

Falling drill
Clip out of your skis and take time to practise simply falling diagonally forwards and down the slope. Make sure you lead with your hips. As you reach your limit, step your leg out to support you.

b

c

Inside-leg drill
Often, your inside leg may be delayed in leaning. To help the hip move earlier in the turn, place your hand inside your thigh as you turn and encourage it to lean and steer to a greater degree.

Use your hand to help activate the inner leg steering.

WATCH IT
see DVD chapter 3

the steering drivetrain

It's essential to have the muscular ability to control leg rotation when steering your skis. Many skiers rotate their legs when initiating turns, but then stay static throughout the rest of the turn. This may be because the skier doesn't know how to steer with the thighs, lacks confidence, relies too much on the skis' sidecut to turn the skis for them, or leans back.

Your muscles should steer your legs through every aspect of a turn. To achieve a better steering action and develop it into a continuous "steering drivetrain", do the pre-ski exercises on pages 40 and 41. These will build endurance in the muscles in your legs, and prepare you for introducing continual leg steering to your turns.

1 Continual leg steering
The left turn has just been completed and the skier has now started leaning his body to begin the right turn.

2 As the legs lean, the thighs steer both skis through the initiation of the turn.

3 The thighs continue steering the skis into the fall line, while the hips and upper body retain their position.

Strength and precision
Building the muscles that steer the legs will enable you to steer more precisely. The weaker the muscles, the less trust you will have in your ability to steer. With more strength, you can use steering in harmony with leg leaning and pressure control, which keeps the turn carving and prevents skidding. This also lets you change the shape of a turn without losing the carve.

4 The skis have now been steered past the fall line. Thigh rotation continues, as more pressure builds on the downhill ski.

5 As the legs progressively lean and the pressure continues to build, the leg steering continues.

6 Keep steering until the end of the turn in order to control your speed, before starting a new turn.

symmetry of your stance

If you want to make clean parallel turns, it's essential that you have a symmetrical stance. This means having your feet, knees, and hips the same distance apart.

There are several reasons why skiers lose the ability to stay in a symmetrical stance when skiing. Lack of confidence can lead to keeping a wider base at the feet, or to dropping the knees inwards. Lack of muscular control may prevent a symmetrical leg position, while poorly fitted ski boots may also contribute to poor leg stance. A good way to improve your leg symmetry is the lateral control exercise.

Symmetrical stance
In a symmetrical stance, feet, knees, and hips are kept the same distance apart, and remain that way throughout your turns. This requires good lateral control.

Pronation
The skier on the left has poor lateral symmetry due to pronation, where the ankles and knees drop inwards. It would be difficult to make good parallel turns in this position, because the skis would be travelling on their inside edges.

Supination
The skier on the right has poor lateral symmetry due to supination, where the ankles and knees drop outwards. Good turns would be difficult because the skis would travel on their outside edges.

1 Lateral control exercise
Both skis should be flat and your bodyweight split 50/50 between your skis. Using your poles for support, begin to slide your feet together.

2 As you slide your skis, make sure that they move equally. Keep your bodyweight evenly distributed and use your poles to support yourself as you do this.

3 Continue sliding the skis until your feet are together. Repeat the exercise until you can feel the leg muscles working that control the lateral movement.

dealing with pressure

To further improve your carved turns, you need to be aware of the pressures on your skis and how you can manage them. Some pressure has to be generated by the skier to bend the ski into a shape that is more effective for carving. Other pressures that build between the skis and the snow need to be managed for efficiency and to prevent your skis skidding at the end of a turn.

1 **Making pressure**
As you move through a turn, you will feel your bodyweight naturally shift towards the rear of the skis.

2 The position of the hips at the end of the turn applies pressure through the tail of the skis. Focus on how you will drive your hips forwards and across to initiate the next turn.

3 Use your arms to help thrust you forwards and diagonally across the skis, so that your hips can move inside the new turn.

Controlling pressure

The pedalling action you learn in the early days of skiing can encourage you to be too abrupt in applying pressure to your skis. At higher speeds, many skiers push too hard on the downhill ski, causing it to skid away. Try to ride the edges and balance on them instead of pushing them away.

Maintaining grip
The skier here is balancing correctly on his edges, riding through the carved turn. The edges are gripping the snow.

Losing grip
The skier here has put too much pressure on his downhill ski, which is not gripping the snow.

4 Maintain the flex in your joints, especially the ankles, as your bodyweight moves forwards and the pressure is applied to the front of the skis.

5 The skis will now be bending under pressure, carving an arc using the reverse camber shape, which is combined with the skis' sidecut.

6 Lean and steer progressively throughout the turn as you feel your bodyweight move towards the tails of the skis again.

WATCH IT
see DVD chapter 3

go steeper

coming up...

Why are steeps more difficult? 120–121

When you stand on a steep slope, it is physically and psychologically different from standing on a relatively flat one. Gravity pulls you down a steep slope faster and you must work harder to control your speed. This may cause you to have your weight over the tails of your skis, which will actually make them harder to steer.

Building confidence: 122–123

You can build your confidence on steeps by using the snowplough wedge shape to begin your turns. You can also check your dynamic stance throughout the turn to make sure that all your joints are flexed and functioning as they would on a relatively flat slope. Make sure you can judge the gradient of the steep and that it runs out to a flatter slope – this also builds confidence.

How to negotiate steeps: 124–125

Using your pole-plant on steeps can improve your skiing technique. Your poles can give you valuable support and also help you to project your body forwards and down the fall line. Specific pole support exercises will develop your ability to do this. Work on these exercises to build your rhythm and flow on steep terrain.

why are steeps more difficult?

The first thing you'll notice when skiing on steeper terrain is that it's more difficult to steer your skis than when on flatter terrain. You'll also notice that when you do manage to change edges and make a turn, your turn accelerates faster than it normally would on a flatter slope. The steeper the slope, the more it will feel like free falling when you turn. This means that you need good balance and greater power to steer your skis.

Most people instinctively lean back when skiing down steeper slopes. However, when you lean back you make the tails of your skis dig harder into the snow. This makes it more difficult to steer your skis. You'll feel the inside ski catch as you turn, causing more acceleration in the fall line. This will make your skiing feel out of control and unpredictable.

Due to the the increase in gravitational pull, you will generally feel heavier when skiing down steeps. You need to be more sensitive to the pressures that build up on your downhill leg – if the forces build up too much, your downhill ski may not be able to hold the edge. The result is that the downhill leg will skid sideways away from you, which can lead to a fall.

WATCH IT see DVD chapter 4

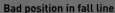

Good position in fall line
When in the fall line, try to keep your weight over the balls of your feet. Keep your ankles flexed and don't let yourself lean back.

Bad position in fall line
Make sure you don't lose the flex in your ankles and allow your body to lag behind your feet. If you lean back, the tails of your skis will dig into the snow, making it harder to steer.

Good position at end of turn
Lean into the slope and grip the snow as you finish the turn, keeping your upper body at a 90° angle to the slope. This gives a firm platform from which to project into the next turn.

Bad position at end of turn
Don't let your upper body fall inside the turn. This will flatten the skis' edge angles and put too much pressure on the uphill ski, allowing the downhill ski to skid away.

building confidence

Building confidence on steep slopes is essential if you want to develop your skiing technique. There are several things you can do to help yourself develop this essential self-belief.

Many skiers lose balance on steeps simply due to lack of confidence. They lean back because they're nervous and lose the flex in their ankle joints. However nervous you may feel, maintain a position that allows you to keep the flex in your ankles. Try to feel and be aware of your ankles flexing throughout your turns.

Another thing you can do to boost your confidence when you first ski steeps is to select terrain that is not far outside your comfort zone. Then work your way up to steeper slopes. Choosing a steep that runs out to a flatter slope means that the end is always in sight, which also boosts confidence.

Finding the right slope
When you're still learning, don't force yourself to tackle the steepest slope you can find. Start in your comfort zone and work your way up to steeper slopes.

1 Using the plough wedge

The start of the turn is the point at which beginners often lack confidence. Use a wedge in order to start the turn comfortably.

2

As you move in the fall line, move your uphill leg out pro-actively into a wedge. Apply pressure to the new downhill ski as you would with the pedalling action in your snowplough turns.

3

Continue to steer through the turn progressively, making sure you complete your turn to control your speed before your next turn.

Good ankle flex
To keep good ankle flex throughout, keep your hips over the balls of your feet as you turn, with your hands out just in front of you.

Bad ankle flex
Don't let your hips drop back behind your feet or extend your ankle joints out straight. With your ankle joints straight, you will lose your leverage and so your power to steer.

WATCH IT
see DVD chapter 4

how to negotiate steeps

To ski parallel on steep slopes, you must be able to move your hips over your feet and down the hill. By doing this, you allow the skis to become flat in relation to the gradient of the slope. When they are flat, they can begin to be steered into the new turn, and as they are steered, they are progressively tilted onto the new edges.

Projecting the hips over the feet and downhill can be a very intimidating feeling on a steep slope. Often, skiers start the steering process before the hips have moved over the feet. When this happens, a snowplough wedge shape is created and the turn will never be completely parallel. To build confidence and practise the movement involved, try using the pole-support drill.

1 Pole-support drill
Plant your pole about 1 metre (3 feet) below your downhill ski, just behind your foot. Place your palm on top of the pole and, keeping your arm relatively straight, allow your bodyweight to rest on the pole.

2
When your weight is being taken by the pole, progressively move your hips across and over your feet. As they move, be sure to keep the weight on the pole. As the skis flatten, steer your legs.

Using your poles

Once you have practised the pole-support drill several times, try to incorporate this feeling into your skiing on steep terrain. As you plant your pole, feel for the movement of your hips over your feet and the flattening of the skis. Once you are in the right position, turning your skis in parallel becomes easy.

Pole-plant
A good pole-plant gives confidence and helps the body to project into the fall line.

3 As you steer with your legs, keep your hips balanced over the balls of your feet. Don't travel across the hill too much – imagine that you are skiing within a corridor that is 2 metres (6 feet) wide.

4 Keep your hips facing down the hill as you complete the turn. Steer your skis across the fall line to stop sliding.

WATCH IT
see DVD chapter 4

go ski moguls

coming up...

Bumps for beginners: 130–131

Moguls are mounds of snow formed by hundreds of skiers riding over the same slope. To ski them well, you need to develop the ability to pivot and skid. This will help you negotiate your line through a mogul field with control. Developing your ability to ski moguls will build your confidence and make your skiing more enjoyable.

Hitting the moguls: 132–133

After developing your ability to skid and pivot your skis, you'll be able to ski moguls with more control. As you get comfortable with moguls, start to challenge yourself by aiming to ski narrower and more direct lines. You can achieve this by further developing your skidding action and studying in more detail the line you are going to take.

Bigger, steeper moguls: 134–135

To develop your mogul skiing further, you can try riding bigger bumps and steeper mogul terrain. To ski these well, you'll need to develop your ability to absorb the moguls while keeping your upper body strong, working the pole-plant and maintaining a closer stance. When you get good at this, you can ski any terrain.

WATCH IT
see DVD chapter 5

bumps for beginners

One of the biggest differences between mogul skiing and piste skiing is that you don't lean your legs laterally so much as you would do when carving. However, if you've never skied moguls before you'll automatically lean your legs when steering. This accelerates you too much for early mogul skiing. To help get a feel for moguls, try turning without leaning. This creates a skidded turn that will help you control your speed in moguls.

1 Braquage turn
To perform linked skidded turns in a narrow corridor, initiate the turns by rotating both thighs.

2 Look at your skis to check they're almost flat to the surface. Continue steering through your thighs, keeping your hips facing down the fall line.

1 Skidded turn
As you initiate the turn, activate thigh steering to rotate your legs without leaning them.

2
Keep your hips over your feet and rotate your thighs. Your hips and shoulders should be facing down the fall line.

3
Allow the skis to skid sideways down the fall line, as you fully rotate the ball of your hip in its socket.

3
Check that your hips are still over your feet, ensuring that your legs aren't leaning laterally. Don't allow your legs to straighten and lose flex.

4
Finish the pivot turn by aiming to steer 90° across the fall line. Repeat this several times in each direction, and try to keep inside a 2-m (6-ft) corridor throughout.

hitting the moguls

To ski a mogul field with control and confidence, use skidded braquage turns. This will control your speed and give you time to find and negotiate a line. Remember, there may be times during your descent when lateral leaning is needed, where the terrain is smoother.

1 Skidding bump to bump
To maintain consistency in your line and speed of descent, rotate your skis on top of the bump, while there is less of the ski touching the ground.

2 As you begin sliding down the backside of the bump, try to skid the skis at right angles to the fall line, so as to control the skidding speed.

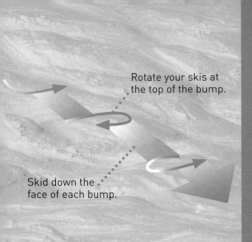

Rotate your skis at the top of the bump.

Skid down the face of each bump.

Finding a line

Most mogul fields have different-sized moguls that can be tackled by everyone from intermediate- to expert-level. Look for consistency in the pattern of the bumps. The easiest place to turn your skis is on the crest of a bump. Once your skis have pivoted, skid down the face of the bump, bring your speed under control, then turn into the next bump.

WATCH IT
see DVD chapter 5

3 As you approach the trough of the next bump, keep your bodyweight in the middle of the skis. Aim your pole-plant at the top of the face of the next bump.

4 As you skid into the face, keep the joints in your legs flexed to absorb any pressure build-up. Firmly plant the pole, preparing to rotate your legs around the next turn.

bigger, steeper moguls

Skiing steeper mogul fields, or ones that have bigger, more cut-out bumps, requires more than just skidding between bumps. To keep control of your speed and line at this level, you need to be able to absorb the moguls. You also need to have a stronger, more activated core, a faster pole-plant, and the ability to hold your stance together laterally.

With bigger bumps, everything happens faster, and if you're off balance you will be punished quickly. Before you enter this type of mogul field, practise the following techniques on bumps you feel comfortable with. Also, it's a good idea to remind yourself of the ankle-flex exercise (see pages 94–95).

Finding the line
Taking a direct line through a steep mogul field (at the top of the picture) requires you to absorb the bumps, ski with a closer stance, and maintain a strong core. Wider turns can be made through gentler areas.

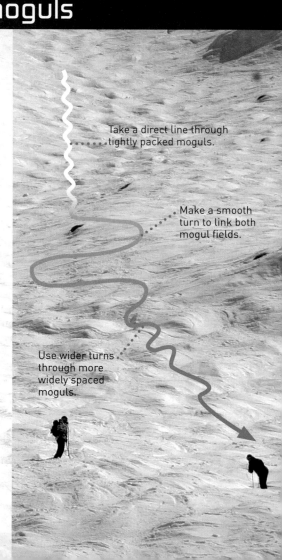

Take a direct line through tightly packed moguls.

Make a smooth turn to link both mogul fields.

Use wider turns through more widely spaced moguls.

Absorbing
This takes the impact out of hitting the face of a mogul. To absorb the bump, pull your feet up under your hips. To extend, push the front of your skis back into the next trough. By extending your legs, you create friction and control your speed.

Strong core and pole-plant
As the impact pressures on your body increase with the size of the moguls, you will need to have a stronger core to avoid your upper body collapsing forwards under the impact and being thrown off balance. The pole-plant also needs to be faster and stronger on bigger moguls.

Feet together
Aim to ski with a closer stance, one that is near a 50/50 distribution of pressure between the skis. Use the lateral control exercise (see pages 112–113) to strengthen your legs on this axis, and keep consistency of pressure in a closer stance.

WATCH IT
see DVD chapter 5

go further

coming up...

Freeskiing: 140–145

Skiing off-piste is one of the most enjoyable aspects of the sport. Freeskiing terrain may encompass a variety of snow conditions, such as powder and snow that's been affected by weather and other skiers on the mountain. Skiing these conditions requires techniques that can be developed on-piste using moguls and steeps, as well as by practising carving.

Freestyle: 146–151

Freestyle skiing has been a major part of the skiing industry since the early 1970s. In recent years, it has grown even bigger with the introduction of twin-tip skis and terrain parks in most resorts. Freestyle skiing gives you a buzz that you won't forget. The basics of freestyle technique include riding switch (backwards), spinning around on your skis, and jumping and grabbing your skis.

what is freeskiing?

The term "freeskiing" describes skiing off-piste. It can be a perfect world of glorious powder snow, but you'll also encounter other snow conditions that are not so ideal, and will place greater demands on your ski technique.

Freeskiing also describes a certain spirit within skiing. This encompasses the incredible silence of the back country, the sensation of your skis floating in powder, and the freedom of skiing your own way in the ultimate outdoor environment.

WATCH IT
see DVD chapter 6

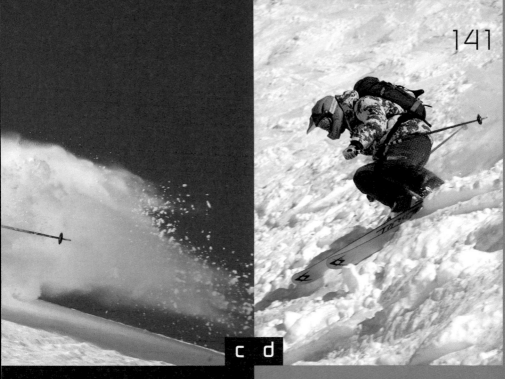

c d

a Weather-affected snow

Powder snow can change due to heat and wind, both of which can create a crusty layer on top of the snow. Notice the large pieces of snow flying in the air.

b Spring snow

Spring (or "corn") snow has been heated and compacted over time. The sun heats the top layer, allowing it to defrost before it freezes again. You'll encounter it after midday, late in the ski season.

c Powder snow

Powder snow is light and easy to ski. It's usually best a day or two after a snow fall. Notice how fine the snow crystals are.

d Chopped-up snow

This type of snow can be technically demanding to ski but is also good for improving and testing your technique. The snow was originally powder but has been skied by hundreds of skiers.

Freeskiing tips

- It's a good idea to adopt a closer stance by keeping your feet closer together. On uneven terrain, a wider stance is actually less stable than a closer one.

- As there are many unpredictable shocks in variable snow conditions, keep your torso rigid. This helps to prevent your body collapsing forwards at the waist.

- Hunched shoulders can also make you vulnerable to collapsing forwards. Raise the height of your shoulders to prevent it.

- Put more pressure into your pole-plant. This allows your body to be supported by the hands as well as the feet, making it feel lighter.

freeskiing for beginners

Powder and variable snow conditions are usually the most challenging for skiers, requiring a higher level of balance, co-ordination, and strength to maintain consistency. In these conditions, you need to adjust your posture and steering to help you ride the terrain with control and fluidity.

There are four main ways you can adjust your position to make sure that you stay balanced and fluid when skiing in powder and variable terrain: stay smooth by steering with the thighs; keep a good balance between your feet; keep your skis closer together than you would when skiing on-piste; and use a firm pole-plant to initiate your turns. This can make it feel as though your hands and feet are touching the snow, giving a "four-wheel drive" element to your skiing.

a

b

Progressive steering
The clean tracks in the snow are evidence that the skier's thighs are steering the skis progressively. Due to pressure of the deep snow, a sudden steering movement would create a large snow wall (see page 145).

Closer stance
A closer stance is best for skiing in powder, as the further apart your skis are, the more they are inclined to travel in different paths. Reduce your usual on-piste stance width by 30 per cent.

Two-footed balance
Because of the unstable nature of the snow surface in powder and variable conditions, you need to have your weight distributed more evenly between your feet. Too much pressure on the downhill ski will make it sink into the snow.

Strong pole-plant
A good pole-plant improves the initiation of turns, and stabilizes your path down variable terrain.

more powder techniques

As you develop your confidence and technique, you will naturally want to freeski at higher speeds. Higher speed freeskiing tests your ability to maintain the basic techniques for freeskiing under more demanding conditions.

When skiing in powder snow at higher speeds, any sudden turns can make it feel as though you're suddenly skiing into a wall of snow. For this reason, you need to keep your turns as rhythmic and fluid as possible. Even so, you are likely to feel much greater pressure than usual building up on your downhill ski. There are techniques that can help you to deal with this, such as retaining tension in your legs, and activating your core muscles to maintain a strong upper-body position.

Skiing in deep powder
Freeskiing terrain is not groomed and solid, but is an ever-changing surface. If you don't control the pressure distribution between your skis, the downhill ski will sink. Retain tension in your legs to maintain an equal distribution of pressure between your skis as you turn. It will never be absolutely equal, but aim for it nevertheless.

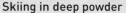

Snow surface
Deep powder is an unpredictable surface to ski on.

Pressure control
To keep turns smooth and progressive requires accurate pressure control.

Leg tension
Retaining tension in the legs helps to keep your skis steering together, even when pressures generated by the turn are forcing them apart.

Turning in deep powder

When you ski in powder at higher speeds, you can feel immense pressure building up under your downhill ski. As you're steering across the fall line, your skis are pushing and compacting the powder snow. This can make the snow feel like a wall of pressure on the outside of your turn, and you have to be careful to prevent your body position from being squashed. When feeling the pressure of this snow wall, the area of the body most vulnerable to folding is the waist. If the middle of the body is weak, the upper body will collapse forwards and you could fall over head first. To avoid this, activate your core muscles and take the pressure through your legs.

Activating your core muscles
To turn in deep powder and withstand the pressure of the snow wall, activate your core.

Riding the snow wall
Pressure from the skis compacts the snow, which creates a snow wall on the outside of the turn.

WATCH IT
see DVD chapter 6

freestyle for beginners

Freestyle skiing has been around since the early 1970s, but over the last decade a new school of freestyle has developed that has given the sport a wider audience. Now most ski resorts have terrain parks. Before you take to the air, you should master the key freestyle skills of skiing switch and the groundspin.

1
How to groundspin
To initiate a groundspin, start rotating the tails of your skis downhill with your thighs.

2
Begin to look around, moving your head in the direction of the rotation. Keep your weight centred.

Head
Always look in the direction in which you are travelling.

Legs
Maintain your leg symmetry so that both skis lie flat.

Hands
The hands should be kept low, like the stance.

Twin-tips
These skis are rounded up at both ends.

WATCH IT
see DVD chapter 6

Skiing switch

To ski switch (backwards), it is best to use special twin-tip skis that have rounded tips and tails so that they can be skied in both directions. On your first attempt, make sure you're on an almost flat gradient and that you can already ski with good leg symmetry. Look over one shoulder to watch out for other skiers.

3 Continue to drive the tails of the skis around, keeping them flat on the snow.

4 When you're halfway through the rotation, start dragging the tips of your skis downhill.

5 Complete the rotation with both skis flat, and the tips aiming down the fall line.

taking your first air

One of the most enjoyable aspects of freestyle skiing is leaving the ground and "taking air time". Jumping is best practised for the first time while skiing on the flat, with the aim of flexing and extending to leave the ground. The technique is the same as it is for jumping off a mound of snow.

Once you've tried this technique a few times and got used to doing it on normal pisted terrain, try it out with the use of a small kicker. A kicker is a small snow ramp that helps you take off. It also has a downhill landing slope to make your landings softer and less jarring to the body.

1 Jumping off a kicker
To begin your approach, stay relaxed and ski up the kicker with good flexibility in all of your joints. Your head should be up and your hands should be out in front of you to aid your balance.

2
As you approach the top of the kicker, progressively extend your legs to "pop" at the take-off of the jump. Be sure that you keep a little flex in your joints throughout the process.

3 As you are travelling through the air, keep your legs flexed. Keep your head up, and look in the direction of your intended landing.

4 As you touch down for landing, make sure that the whole of each ski hits the snow evenly. Ankle flex is essential to remain balanced as you flex to absorb the shock of landing.

WATCH IT
see DVD chapter 6

into the terrain park

Once you become comfortable with jumping and spending time in the air, you can start to practise different types of straight air-jumps. All of these tricks require good balance and a feeling for being in the air, as well as enough elevation in the take-off to give you time to perform them. You can begin testing and developing the balance necessary for these jumps by touching and crossing-up your skis.

a

b

WATCH IT
see DVD chapter 6

Terrain park

Now a standard part of most ski resorts, terrain parks have a range of features, and a grading of green, blue, red, and black descents. Make sure you respect the rights of others, and be careful not to stand in dangerous positions in the park, such as landing areas, runs, and run-outs from the features.

a Hands on boots
To prepare for grabbing your skis, reach down to touch your boots. Be sure to keep your head up, and look forwards.

b "Safety" grab
Reach down with your arm, and pull up with your feet as you get airborne. Grab the outside of the ski edge with your finger and counter-balance with your other arm.

c Crossing skis
Before you try a "critical" grab, try simply crossing the skis while in the air. Leave enough time to return to parallel before you land.

d "Critical" grab
As you reach full height, turn one ski 45° in front of you. Pull up the leg and reach down to grab the ski. Release and return to parallel.

skiing on the net

From resort information to finding out how to get involved in the sport, much of what you need to find out about skiing can be found on the internet.

UK and IRELAND resources

www.skiclub.co.uk
Ski Club of Great Britain is the UK's largest ski club, with the biggest library resource on skiing. The website has a daily news service.

www.ifyouski.com
A valuable resource that offers content on all aspects of skiing. Up-to-date news features and a holiday booking system where you can book a ski holiday from start to finish.

www.warrensmith-skiacademy.com
A coaching organization that trains British skiers in the Alps. The site offers information on the courses run during the winter and summer months, and also has video clips.

www.snowandrock.com
The UK's largest winter outdoor retailer has a wealth of information ski clothing and kit.

www.skiclub.ie
A non-profit organization dedicated to the promotion of skiing in Ireland.

US and CANADA resources

www.powdermag.com
The ultimate inspirational content on the web, with videos, pictures, and stories about some of the best skiing to be found around the world.

www.freeskiers.org
The website of the International Free Skiers Association, with information on US Freeskiing and Skier Cross events. Also has links to other events, athlete listings, and ways of getting involved with freeskiing.

www.ski.com
Everything you need to know about skiing in the US and further afield, from ski technique to ski insurance.

www.skicanada.org
The website of the Canadian Ski Council gives expert advice on the sport and how to participate in it.

AUSTRALIA and NEW ZEALAND resources

www.ski.com.au
Australia's premiere ski information website, covering holidays, technique, and equipment.

www.skiingaustralia.org.au
The website of Ski & Snowboard Australia, the national snowsports association of Australia. Contains the latest athlete information and how to get involved with the sport.

www.snow.co.nz
Extensive coverage of skiing in New Zealand. Holiday bookings, ski resort information, technique tips, weather and snow reports, and even video clips are all here.

www.freeskier.co.nz
This site has up-to-date news and features on freeskiing in New Zealand.

104

ski talk

A-frame stance – skiing with knees closer together than the feet (a bad posture for skiing).

Ankle flex – the ability to flex the ankle joint forwards in the ski boot.

Back country – the untamed areas of the mountain, beyond the boundaries of the piste.

Binding – connects the ski boot to the ski, but allows the boot to release during a fall.

Biomechanics – the mechanical actions of the body while skiing.

Boot flex – bending the boot at the ankle, which is easier in boots with a moveable ankle joint.

Braquage turn – a turn used to slow down, made by steering the skis across the fall line.

Camber – skis that are cambered have a raised profile in the middle of the ski, which makes the ski more pliable and able to follow the snow.

Carving – making a parallel turn to cut a clean arc in the snow, while in a dynamic stance.

Centre of mass – found just above your navel, your centre of mass must be kept over the balls of your feet when you start learning to ski.

Core activation – using the lower back and transverse abdominus muscles while skiing.

Dynamic stance – the body position a skier must aim to maintain in order to balance while on the move.

Edges – the strips of metal running down the sides of the ski base.

Fall line – the line that would be naturally taken by a ball rolling down a slope.

FIS rules – the ten official rules of the International Ski Federation that you should always abide by when skiing.

Freeskiing – a genre of off-piste and all-terrain skiing that symbolizes freedom in the mountains. Also known as freeriding.

Grab – a freestyle move where a skier reaches to grab a part of their skis during a jump.

Inside leg – the leg on the inside of a turn. When a skier is turning left, for example, their left leg is the inside leg.

J-turn – making a snowplough turn that ends with the skis turning slightly back up the hill to feel skidded parallel sensations.

Layering system – wearing several different layers of clothing that keep you warm but allow heat and moisture to disperse.

Moguls – mounds of snow that are created by skiers turning in the same part of the slope.

O-frame – an arm position that promotes a strong upper body.

Outside leg – the leg on the outside of a turn. When a skier is turning left, for example, their right leg is the outside leg.

Parallel turn – turning both skis together so that they remain parallel. Learnt in your first or second week of ski school.

Piste map – a map given out when you buy your lift pass that shows the runs on the mountain.

Pole-plant – planting a ski pole into the ground to aid a turn. Mostly used in high-tempo, short-radius turns.

Pole window – an exercise to avoid upper-body rotation and enhance leg steering.

Pronation – when the feet roll inwards, causing the knees to move together.

Reverse camber – The camber of the ski can be bent into a reverse camber when you stand on the ski, which is useful for carving turns.

Side-slipping – a controlled way of getting down narrow or steep slopes that helps build confidence.

Sidecut – the hourglass shape of most skis, which aids turning.

Skating – a technique similar to inline- or ice-skating, used to move across flat slopes.

Ski school – found in most ski resorts, this is the place for beginner skiers to learn to ski.

Snow wall – the compaction of fresh powder snow as the skier turns across it.

Snowplough – a wedge shape created with your skis that provides basic control and turning capabilities. Learnt in your days of ski school.

Steering drivetrain – a smooth, consistent steering action from the legs, rather than a sudden steering action.

Supination – when the feet roll outwards, making the skier bow-legged.

Switch – skiing backwards. Typically used by freestyle skiers.

Thigh steering – a strong leg-steering action.

Traversing – travelling across a slope on the skis' edges without losing height.

Turn radius – how tightly skis will allow you to turn. Slalom skis have a very small or tight turn radius. Freeride skis have a long turn radius.

PISTE GRADINGS

US, Canada, Australia, New Zealand	Europe	Level of difficulty
●	▬ (green)	Typically a wide, shallow, groomed, beginner slope.
	▬ (blue)	An easy slope, slightly steeper or narrower than a beginner run.
■	▬ (red)	An intermediate slope that is usually groomed.
◆	▬ (black)	An advanced slope, often ungroomed, ranging from terrain that is just beyond intermediate level, to expert terrain such as steep chutes and drops.
◆◆		

index